the Moon

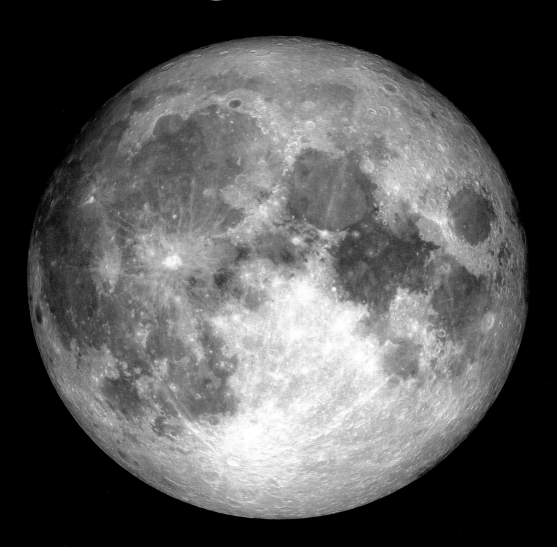

Project Editor Sophie Parkes
Senior Art Editor Rachael Parfitt Hunt
Senior US Editor Shannon Beatty
Editor Sarah MacLeod
Designer Sif Nørskov
Additional Design Robert Perry
Jacket Design Claire Patane
Jacket Co-ordinator Issy Walsh
Senior Picture Researcher Sakshi Saluja
Assistant Picture Researcher Mayank Choudhary
Senior Producer, Pre-Production Dragana Puvacic
Producer Inderjit Bhullar
Managing Editor Penny Smith
Deputy Art Director Mabel Chan
Publishing Director Sarah Larter

Written by Dr. Sanlyn Buxner, Dr. Georgiana Kramer, Dr. Pamela Gay
Illustrated by Dawn Cooper
Contributors Larry Lebofsky, Maria Banks, Andrea Jones,
Andrew Shaner, Mathew Wenger, Rob Bovill

First American Edition, 2022
Published in the United States by DK Publishing
1745 Broadway, 20th Floor, New York, NY 10019
Copyright © 2022 Dorling Kindersley Limited
DK, a Division of Penguin Random House LLC
22 23 24 25 26 10 9 8 7 6 5 4 3 2 1
001–326081–Nov/2022

A catalog record for this book
is available from the Library of Congress.
ISBN 978-0-7440-5659-4

DK books are available at special discounts when purchased
in bulk for sales promotions, premiums, fund-raising, or educational use. For
details, contact: DK Publishing Special Markets,
1745 Broadway, 20th Floor, New York, NY 10019
SpecialSales@dk.com

Printed and bound in China

For the curious
www.dk.com

This book was made with Forest
Stewardship Council™ certified paper –
one small step in DK's commitment to a
sustainable future. For more information
go to www.dk.com/our-green-pledge

Contents

WELCOME TO THE MOON

The Moon is our nearest neighbor and the only world beyond our own that humans have walked on.

People all around the world have been trying to understand the Moon for thousands of years. They began by carefully watching it, then mapping it using telescopes, then sending spacecraft to see it up close. Eventually, they touched and explored its surface with people and robotic spacecraft. Even now, we are learning new things about the Moon all the time.

In this book, we explore our connection to this amazing celestial object, take a look at lunar exploration, and dream about humans returning to the Moon one day in the future.

As you learn about the Moon, here are some useful terms to keep in mind...

Useful things to know:

astronaut
A person who works in outer space

celestial body
An object that is found in space, such as a star, planet, or moon

crater
A hole in the ground made by a rock falling from space

dwarf planet
A small celestial body that is smaller than a planet, bigger than an asteroid, orbits the Sun, and isn't a moon

gravity
An invisible force that pulls objects toward each other

lunar
Anything to do with the Moon

mare
A dark region on the Moon made from ancient lava flows. Several regions are called maria

moon
A natural satellite that orbits a planet or asteroid—our Moon is only one of them!

meteoroid
A solid rock that is in space—it can be any size or shape

orbit
The path in space an object, such as a planet or moon, takes around another object

planet
A big, round object, such as Earth, that orbits a star, such as our Sun. Planets that go around other stars are called extrasolar planets

satellite
An object that orbits something other than a star—the Moon is a natural satellite and spacecraft are artificial satellites

solar system
A system of planets, moons, and other small bodies that orbit a star such as our Sun. There are planetary systems around other stars as well

star
A glowing ball of gas that gives off its own light

Sun
The star in the center of our solar system

Where is the Moon?

The Moon and Earth are part of a diverse family of objects that orbit our Sun, which together forms the solar system. Planets come in many sizes, and most of them have moons—Saturn has more than 80 moons! The solar system also includes smaller icy and rocky objects such as comets, asteroids, and dwarf planets.

Inner planets

The four inner planets are solid worlds, which means that you can stand on them. They are called terrestrial planets and include Mercury, Venus, Earth, and Mars.

Moon

Sun

Mercury   Venus   Earth   Mars

Our home, Earth, is the third planet from the Sun, after Mercury and Venus.

Jupiter

Most asteroids (small, rocky objects that orbit the Sun) orbit between Mars and Jupiter. However, additional space rocks can be found everywhere in the solar system—some even became moons of Jupiter and Saturn.

Earth

From Earth...

Our Earth is pretty big. Its diameter (distance across the middle) is 7,917 miles (12,742 km).

The worlds here are not to scale. If they were, you wouldn't be able to see the smallest planets or fit them on a single page! Space is very big, and it is mostly empty.

Outer planets

The outer planets are gas planets, which means they do not have solid surfaces. Humans would need balloons or flying vehicles to explore their colorful gases. These planets, which include Jupiter, Saturn, Uranus, and Neptune, have many moons.

Uranus

Neptune

Saturn

Comets are icy celestial balls that orbit the Sun They come from the very edge of the solar system.

Inner planets

Jupiter   Saturn   Uranus   Neptune

The lines on this diagram show how far the planets are relative to one another (although they're not found in a line).

Moon

...to the Moon

The Moon is around 238,900 miles (384,500 km)—or 30 Earths—away from us. The Apollo astronauts took over 3 days traveling at around 2,000 mph (3,280 kph) to get there.

Moon vs. Earth

The Moon is Earth's nearest neighbor. These two rocky worlds have a lot in common, which we will explore in this book, but here are some of the differences between them.

Moon

The Moon is smaller than Earth, and has less mass.

Diameter

With a diameter of 2,159 miles (3,475 km), the Moon is much smaller than Earth. In fact, nearly four Moons would fit across Earth's face.

Diameter is the distance from edge to edge through the middle of a circle or sphere.

Volume

The volume of Earth is so much greater than that of the Moon that a whopping 50 Moons would fit inside Earth if it were hollow!

Earth's volume is 260 billion cubic miles (1,083 billion km³).

The Moon's volume is 5 billion cubic miles (22 billion km³).

A year

Earth is a planet that orbits the Sun. The Moon is a satellite that orbits Earth. A year on Earth is the time it takes to go completely round the Sun, which is 365 Earth days. A year is the same on the Moon, as it travels with Earth.

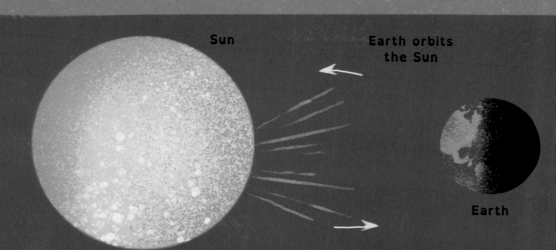

Sun

Earth orbits the Sun

Earth

Astronaut

Hottest:
136°F (58°C)
Coldest:
-126°F (-88°C)

Earth

Moon

Hottest:
260°F (127°C)
Coldest:
-280°F (-173°C)

Earth

Temperature

Earth's atmosphere protects us from the Sun's heat and cold outer space, but the Moon experiences extreme hot and cold temperatures.

Gravity

Earth has a much greater mass than the Moon, which means its force of gravity is much stronger. You would weigh about one-sixth of your Earth weight on the Moon, so you could jump much higher.

A person can jump six times higher on the Moon than on Earth.

The things in these diagrams are not to scale!

Moon

Earth and the Moon rotate on their axes as they orbit the Sun. Earth rotates faster than the Moon.

Earth

A day

One day is the time between two Sunrises. The Sun rises and sets as Earth rotates. A day on Earth is 24 hours, and a day on the Moon is much longer— 29.5 Earth days.

Forming the Moon

The Moon formed around 4.5 billion years ago, when two planets, Theia and Gaia, crashed into each other. The fragments of rock and dust that were sprayed into space by the collision later merged to form an object we now know as the Moon.

Scientists have made models of the impact, making Theia different sizes, to try to understand what happened.

Over time, Gaia's gravity tugs Theia, a planet about the same size as Mars, toward it.

Theia

Gaia

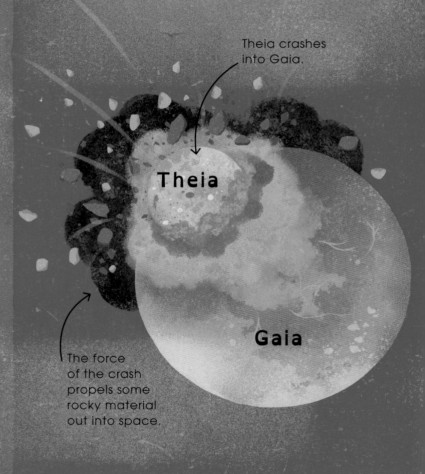

Theia crashes into Gaia.

Theia

Gaia

The force of the crash propels some rocky material out into space.

Doomed from the start

Gaia and Theia form much too close to each other in the young solar system. Their gravitational attraction to each other means the planets are destined to meet.

Crash!

Theia collides with Gaia. The metal cores from both planets merge, and most of the rocky materials mix together to become the planet we call Earth.

One of the aims of the Apollo missions (which landed humans on the Moon) was to figure out how the Moon formed.

Rock and soil brought back from the Moon by the Apollo missions allowed scientists to figure out the theory you see here.

Heavy materials, such as iron and nickel, from both planets begin to form a core at the center of the planet we now call Earth.

Earth

Rocky debris

The rocky material forms a ring that orbits Earth.

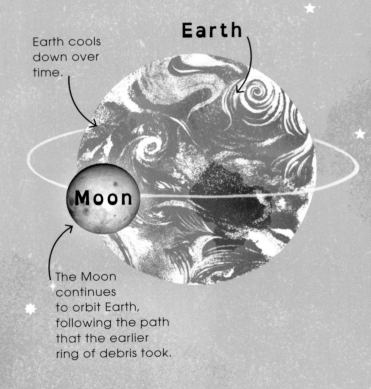

Earth cools down over time.

Earth

Moon

The Moon continues to orbit Earth, following the path that the earlier ring of debris took.

A rocky ring forms

Some of the rocky material from both planets is flung into space by the impact. Earth's gravity pulls these rock fragments and dust into a ring that orbits around it.

The Moon forms

The ring of rocky fragments is pulled together by its own gravity into a ball of melted rock. It slowly cools to form the young Moon.

Other moons in the solar system

Earth has just one moon, which we call the Moon. But there are hundreds of other moons all over our solar system. These moons orbit other planets, dwarf planets, and even asteroids. They come in a variety of sizes and shapes, and are made of many different combinations of materials.

The moons on this page are not to scale!

Ganymede

Jupiter's moon Ganymede has a diameter of 3,270 miles (5,262 km), making it the largest moon in the solar system. It's bigger than the planet Mercury!

Titan

One of Saturn's moons, Titan has a diameter of 3,200 miles (5,149 km), a thick atmosphere, and liquid lakes.

Callisto

Callisto orbits Jupiter and has a diameter of 2,995 miles (4,821 km). It has a lot of craters on its surface.

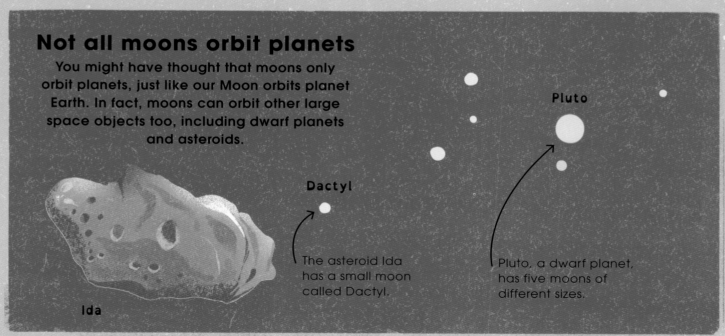

Not all moons orbit planets

You might have thought that moons only orbit planets, just like our Moon orbits planet Earth. In fact, moons can orbit other large space objects too, including dwarf planets and asteroids.

Dactyl

Pluto

The asteroid Ida has a small moon called Dactyl.

Pluto, a dwarf planet, has five moons of different sizes.

Ida

Not all moons are round

While Earth's Moon is spherical in shape, small moons can look a lot like the rocks you might find in your yard. These moons are not big enough to be round.

Pan

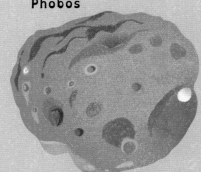

Deimos

Phobos

Mars has two tiny, oddly shaped moons called Deimos and Phobos.

Saturn has moons shaped a little like ravioli! This one is called Pan.

The Moon

The Moon is Earth's only natural satellite, or moon. It is less than a third of the size of Earth, with a diameter of 2,159 miles (3,476 km).

Io

Jupiter's moon Io is a world of huge volcanoes— hundreds of them pepper its surface. It has a diameter of 2,264 miles (3,643 km).

Europa

Jupiter's moon Europa has an enormous sea hidden beneath its icy surface. This moon's diameter is 1,940 miles (3,122 km).

Record-breaking moons

Earth's Moon is only the fifth largest in the solar system. The largest moons orbit the largest planets: Jupiter and Saturn. These planets also have more moons orbiting them than any other planet.

CHAPTER 1

OUR CONNECTION TO THE MOON

The Moon is familiar to all of us, and it has been important to humans for a very long time.

We see it often in the sky, and it follows predictable patterns as it rises and sets. Before humans knew much about the Moon, we told stories about this mysterious object. In this section, you will explore the ways the Moon is connected to us, from how it affects nature on Earth to the incredible ways we can see it in the sky.

The lunar light

Why does the Moon appear to change shape? The Moon doesn't create its own light, so what we see when we look at the Moon is just the reflection of light from the Sun lighting one side of the Moon. As the Moon orbits Earth, we see more or less of the lit side.

As the lit area grows, the Moon is said to be "waxing,"

Waxing cresent

First quarter

Waxing gibbous

Full Moon

Phases of the Moon

As the Moon travels around Earth, it appears—but only appears—to change shape from night to night. These shapes are known as the phases of the Moon, or the lunar cycle.

Sea turtles

Some scientists believe that sea turtles come out of the sea to nest when the Moon is darkest.

Changing shapes

These different shapes of the Moon are called phases. It takes 29.5 days for the Moon to go through them all. A new Moon is when we cannot see the Moon lit up.

and as it appears to shrink, it is called "waning."

Waning gibbous

Third quarter

Waning cresent

New Moon

The lunar cycle

The Moon is constantly orbiting Earth. The side of the Moon facing the Sun is lit up. On Earth, how much we can see of the lit side of the Moon changes each day, depending on where the Moon is in its orbit.

Earth's axis

Moon's axis

Moon's orbit

The Earth and Moon spin on their axes.

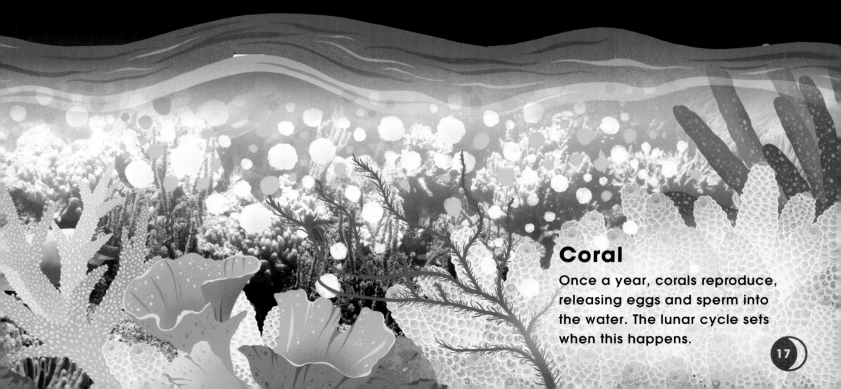

Coral

Once a year, corals reproduce, releasing eggs and sperm into the water. The lunar cycle sets when this happens.

The Moon over a month

The Moon is so bright in the night sky that it is easy to notice. In fact, over the course of a month, the Moon is up in the sky during the day as much as it is during the night. The time the Moon is in the sky, and its phase, are different each day. Here is the time of day you can see each phase high in the sky over a month.

Each day is different

The time you can see the Moon each day changes depending on the phase it is in. This is because the Moon rises about 50 minutes later each day as it travels around Earth. This changes how much we see of the lit-up side each day.

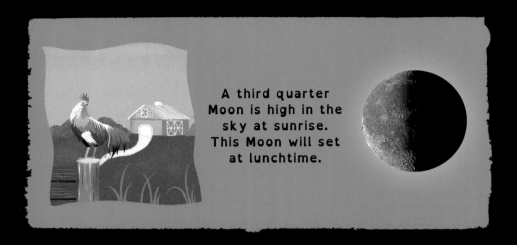

A third quarter Moon is high in the sky at sunrise. This Moon will set at lunchtime.

A waning crescent Moon is high in the morning and is seen during the day.

Keep your eyes peeled for the Moon in the sky, whether it is day or night!

A waxing crescent Moon is high in the sky when school finishes mid-afternoon.

A first quarter Moon is highest in the sky around dinnertime and sets late at night.

A waxing gibbous Moon is high in the evening. As the Moon moves around Earth, we see more and more of it lit up.

A full Moon is high in the sky at midnight. It rises near Sunset, and sets near Sunrise.

The full Moon

A full Moon is when the whole side of the Moon that is lit up by the Sun can be seen from Earth. This happens when the Moon and Sun are on opposite sides of Earth to each other.

Everyone sees the same Moon

Over the course of one day, everyone on Earth will see the same Moon in the same phase. But not everyone will see it the same way up or at the exact same time. How the Moon appears to be rotated in the sky will depend on where in the world you look at it from.

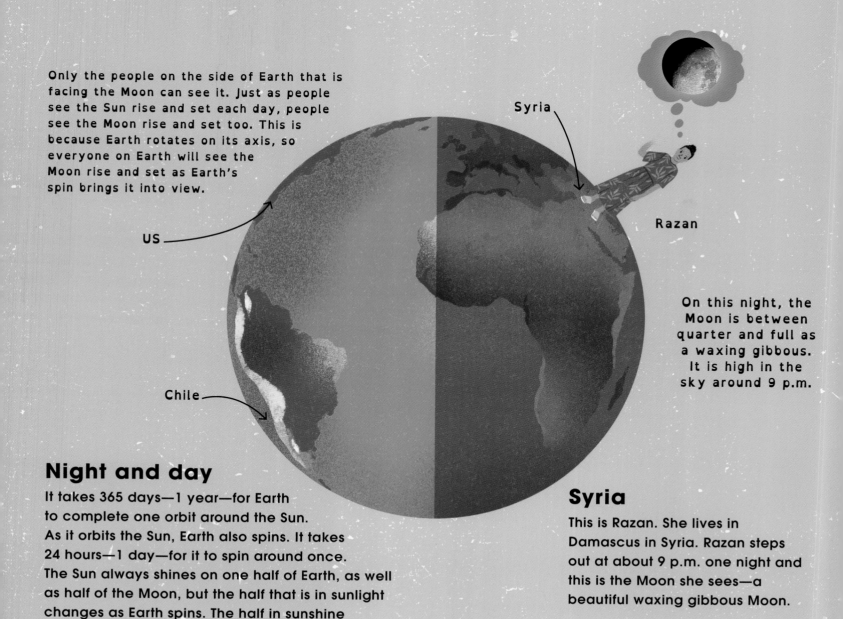

Only the people on the side of Earth that is facing the Moon can see it. Just as people see the Sun rise and set each day, people see the Moon rise and set too. This is because Earth rotates on its axis, so everyone on Earth will see the Moon rise and set as Earth's spin brings it into view.

US

Chile

Syria

Razan

On this night, the Moon is between quarter and full as a waxing gibbous. It is high in the sky around 9 p.m.

Night and day

It takes 365 days—1 year—for Earth to complete one orbit around the Sun. As it orbits the Sun, Earth also spins. It takes 24 hours—1 day—for it to spin around once. The Sun always shines on one half of Earth, as well as half of the Moon, but the half that is in sunlight changes as Earth spins. The half in sunshine experiences daytime, meanwhile the half in darkness experiences nighttime.

Syria

This is Razan. She lives in Damascus in Syria. Razan steps out at about 9 p.m. one night and this is the Moon she sees—a beautiful waxing gibbous Moon.

Every person on Earth is held to the ground by a force called gravity. Because Earth is a sphere, people standing on one side of the planet are upside down compared to people on the other side. And they see the Moon upside down, too!

United States

This is Billy. He lives in Virginia Beach. Night arrives here about 12 hours after it does for Razan in Syria. When Billy steps outside and looks up at the Moon, it looks the same as Razan's Moon.

Billy

Chile

This is Camila. She lives in Concepción in Chile. She looks at the Moon at about the same time as Billy, but this is what she sees when she looks up into the sky. The Moon is tilted compared to how it is for Billy and Razan!

Chile

Camila

Syria is out of sight round the other side of Earth as Earth has rotated.

Why does the Moon look different?

Around the middle of Earth is an imaginary line called the equator. It divides Earth into two halves, known as hemispheres. The Moon that Camila sees in Chile is opposite way up to Billy's Moon. This is because she is looking at it from the Southern Hemisphere, below Earth's equator. People in the Southern Hemisphere are standing upside down compared to people in the Northern Hemisphere!

Syria is in the Northern Hemisphere.

The US is in the Northern Hemisphere.

Northern Hemisphere

Equator

Southern Hemisphere

Chile is in the Southern Hemisphere.

Solar eclipses

Several times a year, the Moon moves directly between Earth
and the Sun, and casts a tiny shadow onto Earth. If you are in the
shadow and look up, the Sun will appear to be covered by the Moon.
This is called a solar eclipse. Not all eclipses look the same.
Sometimes the whole Sun is blocked by the Moon, and sometimes
only part of the Sun is covered, leaving a ring or slice of sunlight.

Different eclipses

A total solar eclipse is when the whole Sun appears to be covered by the Moon.
When you see just a part of the Sun covered up, it is called a partial solar eclipse.
Below is a sequence of the other type of solar eclipse, called an annular eclipse.
This is when a thin ring of sunlight can be seen around the Moon as it passes in front of the Sun.

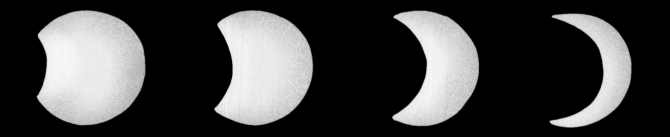

How it works

Everything in the solar system is on a slight tilt,
which means amazing things can happen
depending on how those tilts line up. This model
shows the relative order of the Sun, Moon, and
Earth when a solar eclipse occurs—the Moon is
between the Sun and Earth. People in the shadow
of the Moon on Earth get to see the eclipse.

Telescope projector

Watching solar eclipses

You must never, ever look directly at the Sun or a solar eclipse without protecting your eyes. An adult may be able to show you how to project the Sun onto paper using a telescope. Or you can buy special solar glasses, with protective solar filters. These are different from regular sunglasses and make it safe to look at the Sun. Ask an adult for help.

Solar glasses

! NEVER LOOK DIRECTLY AT THE SUN

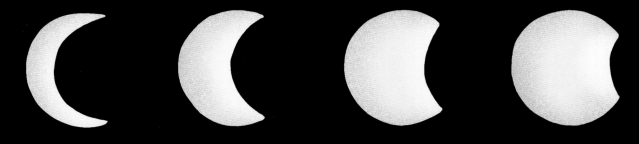

This is just a model and is not to scale in size or distance.

Sun

Moon

Earth

The Moon passes between Earth and the Sun.

Lunar eclipses

The Moon and the Sun have been used to track the passage of days and seasons for as long as humans have been recording history. Along with the normal cycle of the Moon, from full Moon to new Moon, one to three times a year a full Moon makes a surprising change—it turns dark gray or deep red. While people considered this a scary sign in ancient times, we now understand that it is simply what happens when the Moon dips into Earth's shadow.

How it works

The Moon's orbit is tilted a little, and most months it travels above or below Earth's shadow. But several times a year, when the Moon's orbit aligns just right, the Moon travels through Earth's shadow, causing a lunar eclipse. This model shows the relative order of the Sun, Earth, and Moon during a lunar eclipse.

Eclipsed Moon

The part of the Moon that is covered by Earth's shadow will turn dark gray or red, depending on what is in Earth's air. When the air contains a lot of smoke or volcanic ash, the Moon appears more red. Other times, it is dark gray.

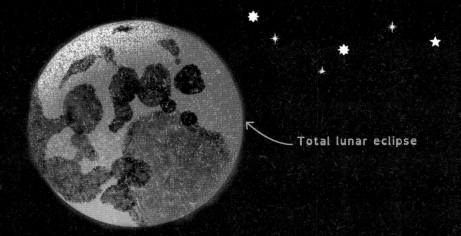

Total lunar eclipse

A lunar eclipse only occurs during a full Moon.

Total and partial eclipses

When the Moon is entirely in the shadow of Earth, it is called a total eclipse. If the Moon only partly moves into Earth's shadow, it is known as a partial eclipse. In a partial eclipse, only part of the Moon turns red or gray, and the rest is white.

It is completely safe to look at a lunar eclipse.

This is just a model and is not to scale in size or distance.

Earth comes between the Moon and the Sun.

Sun

Earth

Moon

Earth spins on its axis once every day. As it turns, the gravitational pulls of the Moon and the Sun create either high or low tides. The side of Earth closest to the Moon and the side farthest away from the Moon experience high tides. The sides not in line with the Moon have low tides.

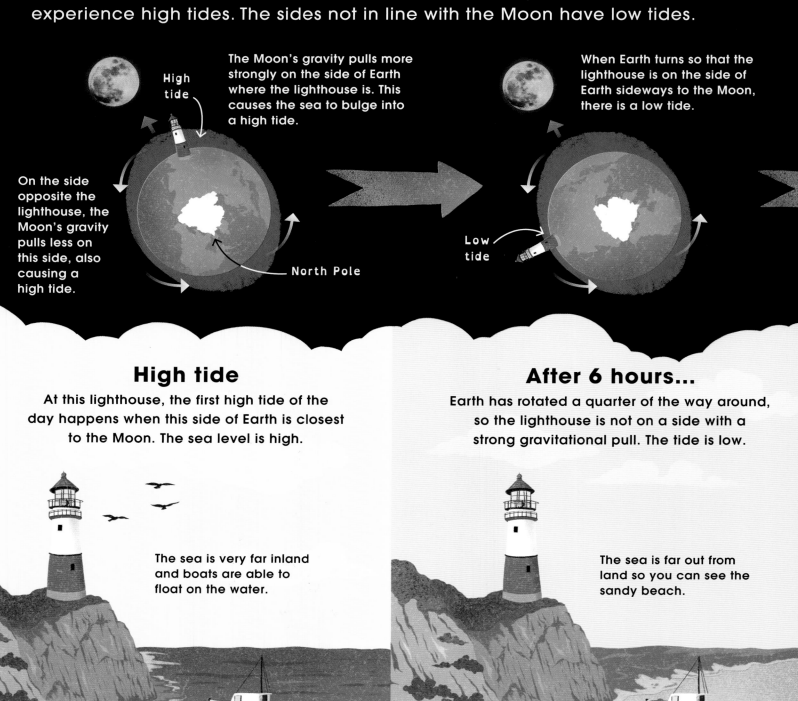

The Moon's gravity pulls more strongly on the side of Earth where the lighthouse is. This causes the sea to bulge into a high tide.

High tide

On the side opposite the lighthouse, the Moon's gravity pulls less on this side, also causing a high tide.

North Pole

When Earth turns so that the lighthouse is on the side of Earth sideways to the Moon, there is a low tide.

Low tide

High tide

At this lighthouse, the first high tide of the day happens when this side of Earth is closest to the Moon. The sea level is high.

The sea is very far inland and boats are able to float on the water.

After 6 hours...

Earth has rotated a quarter of the way around, so the lighthouse is not on a side with a strong gravitational pull. The tide is low.

The sea is far out from land so you can see the sandy beach.

The way the Moon's gravitational pull causes high and low tides is called a tidal force.

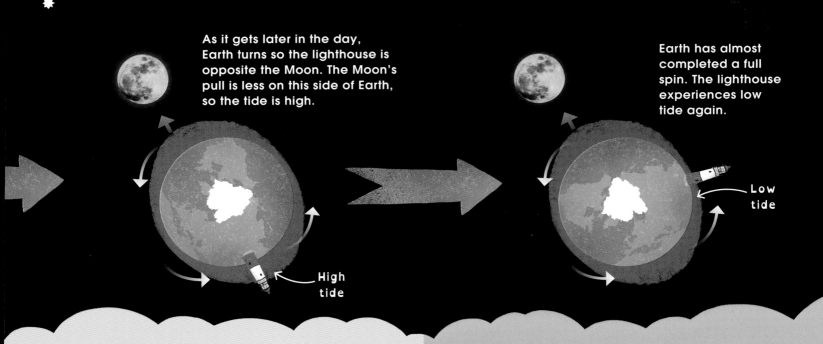

As it gets later in the day, Earth turns so the lighthouse is opposite the Moon. The Moon's pull is less on this side of Earth, so the tide is high.

High tide

Earth has almost completed a full spin. The lighthouse experiences low tide again.

Low tide

After 12 hours...

By this point, Earth has spun halfway. The lighthouse is on the side opposite the Moon, where the tidal force is least strong. This allows the tide to rise up again.

The sea is closer to the shore again. The second high tide in some places has a lower sea level than the first.

After 18 hours...

Earth has spun three-quarters of the way by now. It's getting darker as the day is ending, and the tide is low once again.

The boat gets stuck in the sand when the sea level is low.

Finding shapes on the Moon

Humans have been looking at the Moon for thousands of years, trying to find patterns in the dark areas—the maria—etched across its face. Over the centuries, people have created many stories, legends, and myths about the shapes they see.

The Moon spins while it orbits Earth. But the weird thing is, the time it takes the Moon to spin around once is exactly the same time it takes to orbit Earth—about 27 and a half days! This means that the same side of the Moon is always facing Earth—the lunar nearside. The side that faces away from Earth is called the lunar farside.

This is the lunar nearside.

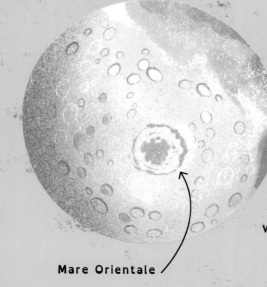

Mare Orientale

Which side?

On Earth, we only ever see the nearside of the Moon, so most of our stories about the Moon relate to the features on this side. On the western side is a crater called Mare Orientale, which is difficult to see from Earth. What stories do you think we would have told if this had been the side looking down at Earth every night?

One of the most common things people say they can see on the Moon is a person's face!

You can see lots of craters and maria on the nearside.

What do you see on the Moon?

If you look carefully, there are lots of different shapes you can make out of the Moon's maria. Here are some ideas, but you might see something completely different!

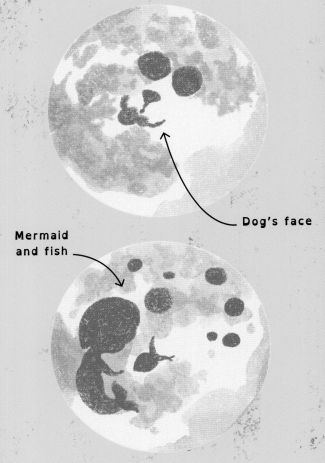

Dog's face

Mermaid and fish

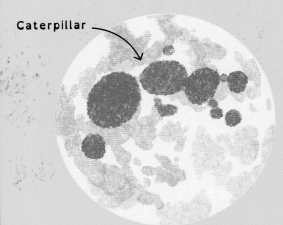

Caterpillar

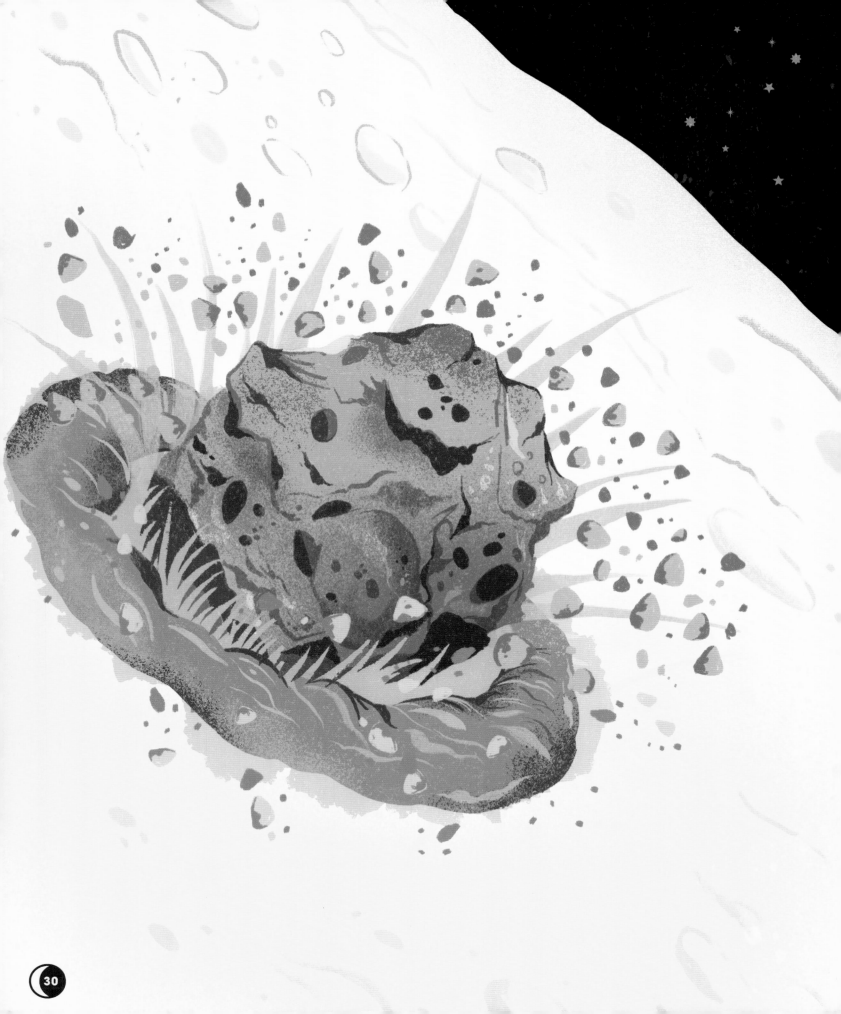

CHAPTER 2

FEATURES ON THE MOON

Humans have been looking at the Moon for thousands of years, but we are learning new things about it every day.

In this section, we will explore the amazing features of the Moon, from epic craters to ancient erupting volcanoes. You will discover parts of it that can been seen with just your eyes, and other parts that we have discovered using telescopes, cameras, and spacecraft.

What is the Moon made of?

When it first formed, the Moon's surface was made of hot, molten rock. At first, the lighter, brighter rock floated to the surface. But over a long period of time, darker rock seeped up through cracks in the surface, giving the Moon its beautiful darker areas.

Each dark area on the Moon is called a mare. Lots of areas are called maria.

Mare

Astronomers once thought that the dark areas on the surface could be oceans. "Mare" is Latin for "sea."

Basalt from the maria

Maria

The dark rock of the maria is called basalt. This rock is not just found on the Moon—it can be found all over the solar system's inner planets: Mercury, Venus, Earth, and Mars. It is the same rock that erupts from volcanoes on Earth's Hawaiian Islands and Galápagos Islands.

The bright areas are called the highlands.

Highland

Highlands

The bright areas of the Moon's surface are called the highlands. They are made of a rock called anorthosite. On Earth, anorthosite can be found in granite and is often used to make statues.

Scientists are still studying rocks brought back by the Apollo missions in the 1960s and 1970s.

Anorthosite from the highlands

Some rocks contain a rare mineral that was found on the Moon before it was found on Earth. It was discovered in rocks collected by the Apollo 11 mission in 1969. Scientists named the mineral armalcolite, after the astronauts on that mission: Armstrong, Aldrin, and Collins.

Contrary to what some fairy tales might say, it's a myth that the Moon is made of cheese.

The Moon is not made of cheese!

What are craters?

Rocks from space are constantly bombarding the surface of the Moon, as well as other rocky bodies in the solar system, and making holes. These holes are called craters.

Rocks of all sizes

Planets such as Earth have an atmosphere, which burns or breaks up space objects that enter it—only large solid rocks survive to reach Earth's surface. However, the Moon has no atmosphere, so rocks of all sizes, from as small as a speck of dust to bigger than a house, make it to the surface and form craters.

Often, rocks from space land on top of craters. There are lots of places on the Moon where you can see craters on top of other craters!

Meteoroids, meteors, and meteorites

You may be wondering what the difference is between these three words. They describe the same space rock, but at different stages of its journey.

- The rock is a meteoroid while it's traveling in space.
- It's a meteor as it burns or breaks up going through an atmosphere. There are no meteors on the Moon since there is no atmosphere.
- If any of it is left after it hits the surface, it's called a meteorite.

Meteoroids hit the Moon all the time!

Craters everywhere!

There are so many craters on the Moon that it would be impossible to count them. The Moon doesn't have an atmosphere, which means there is no wind, rain, or snow to blow or wash them away. Once a crater is made, it may never disappear. In fact, the only way the Moon's surface gets weathered is by other craters being made! This is one of the reasons there are many more craters on the Moon than on Earth.

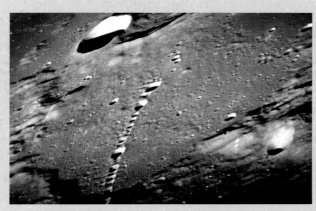

Sometimes asteroids or comets break into pieces and create a crater chain—a line of craters that are formed as all the pieces of the asteroid hit the surface.

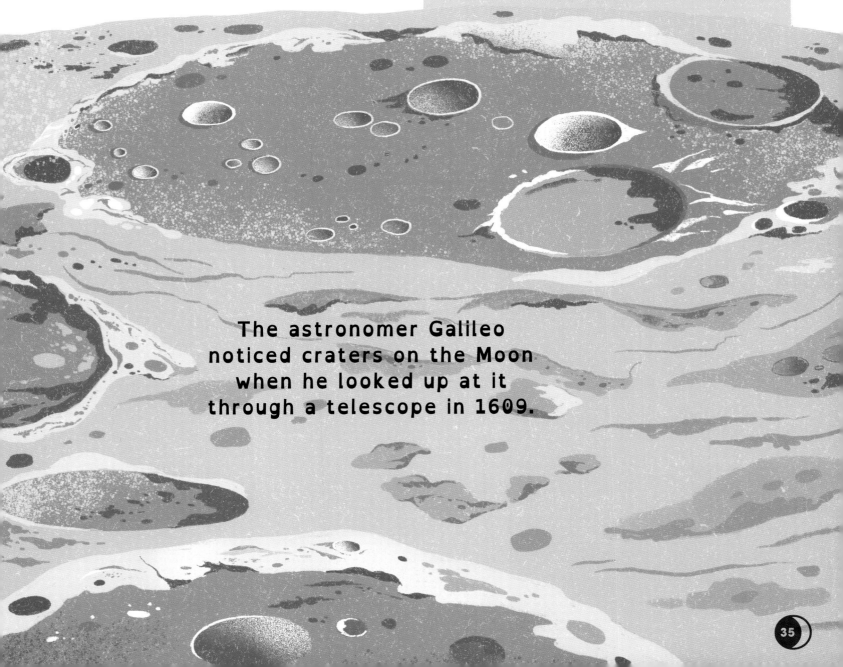

The astronomer Galileo noticed craters on the Moon when he looked up at it through a telescope in 1609.

How simple craters form

Most of the craters seen on the Moon and other rocky bodies in the solar system are known as simple craters. This is because they are simple, bowl-shaped dents in the ground.

1

Space rock incoming!

A meteoroid is on a collision course with the Moon. It is a meteoroid because it is traveling in space.

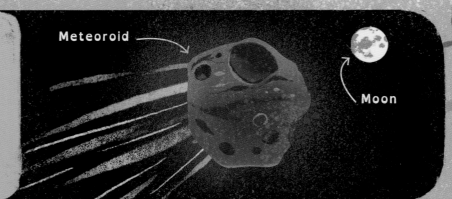

Meteoroid

Moon

2

Meteoroid hits surface.

Shock waves

The meteoroid hits

The meteoroid is traveling very fast when it crashes into the surface of the Moon. The force of the collision sends vibrations, or shock waves, into the ground.

A glimpse under the surface

Craters allow humans to see what is under the surface of the Moon, without needing to interfere by touching it or digging it up. That's because the explosion makes the surface layers flip over, like opening a book—the pages under the book cover are now on top of the book cover.

3

It explodes

The energy from this collision causes a huge explosion that breaks apart the meteoroid and blasts a hole in the Moon's surface. Pieces of lunar crust and meteorite fly up and out in all directions. This debris is called ejecta.

Ejecta

Surface layers flip over.

4

A crater is formed on the Moon's surface.

A hole is left

The surface cools, and a simple crater is left behind where the meteoroid hit. This crater will remain on the Moon for many millions of years.

Basin formation

When a space rock strikes the lunar surface, it sends energy into the ground. The bigger the rock, the greater the amount of energy it sends. Shock waves travel through the ground, which can make it behave a bit like water.

Rock is thrown up and out from the impact.

When a crater is too big to stay a simple shape, it is called a complex crater.

The biggest craters are called multi-ring basins, because the crater is surrounded by rings.

Shock waves from the impact travel through the ground.

Complex craters are formed by bigger rocks from space.

Rippling rock

The rings that form around basin craters are a little like the ripples you see when you drop a pebble into water. At first, the pebble creates a dip in the surface. Then rings ripple outward, getting larger as they move away from the center. Impacts on the Moon's surface work in a similar way. If an impact is strong enough, the rock surrounding it can behave like water!

Big craters

The largest craters are called basins. They make huge dents in the Moon's crust and are surrounded by ring after ring of uplifted rock. Most lunar basins were filled with lava, so these rings cannot be seen anymore. But this is not the case for all of them! Mare Orientale looks like a bull's-eye since lava only filled its center, meaning its rings of rock are still visible.

The crater rebounds

If the energy from the meteoroid is strong enough, the ground at the center of the crater can rebound (come back up).

The rebounding ground forms a peak at the center.

Moon

Tycho crater's central peak

The peak collapses

If the meteoroid is enormous, the central peak will collapse, causing ripples in the rock to travel outward.

The peak collapses back down.

Ripples in the rock travel out from the center.

Moon

Mare Orientale's rings of rock

Features to spot

The Moon is often the brightest object in the night sky. It's also the closest celestial body to us on Earth, which means it is easy to observe with the naked eye or a telescope. Beautiful features and formations cover its surface, and you can look for and admire them yourself.

1 Copernicus crater

2 Lunar swirl

3 Tycho crater

4 Sea of Tranquility

The Moon shines brightly in the sky, but it has no light of its own—it reflects the light from the Sun.

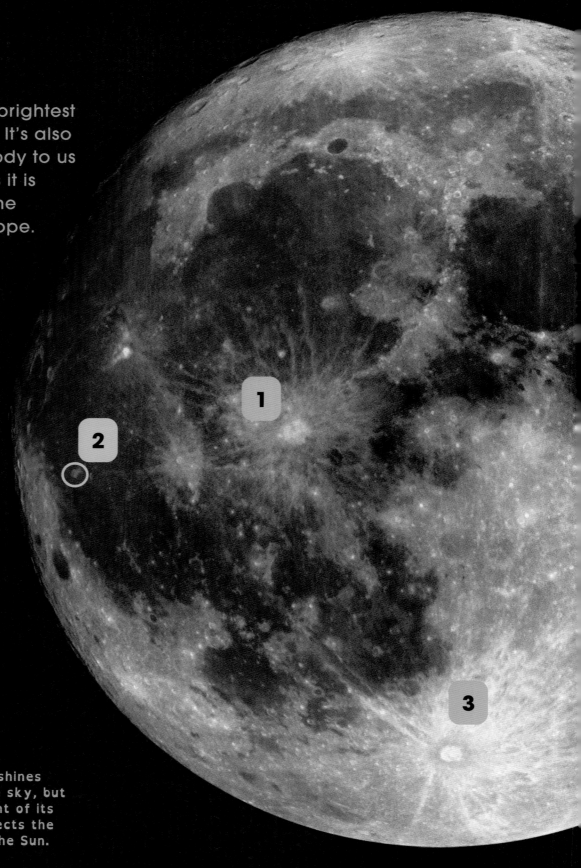

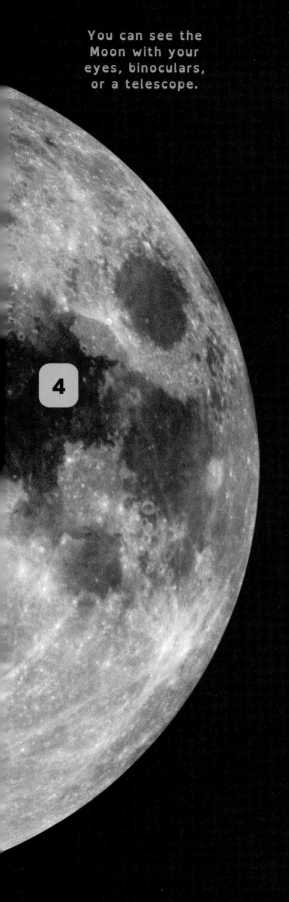

You can see the Moon with your eyes, binoculars, or a telescope.

4

See for yourself!

The next time it is a clear, dry night, why don't you go and do some moongazing? There are all sorts of fascinating features to spot on the Moon's surface, from vast mountain ranges to deep valleys and huge craters. Here are some interesting features to find. Can you see them?

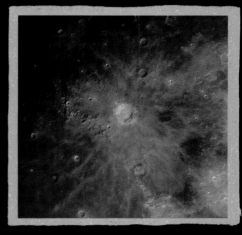

Copernicus crater

You will be able to see this crater with your eyes, binoculars, or a telescope. The rays were caused by material spraying out when the crater was created.

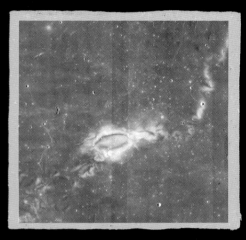

Lunar swirl

Spot these strange features with a telescope. Scientists don't know much about them—they think the swirls are patterns of Moondust protected by a magnetic field.

Tycho crater

This huge crater, also with long rays, is thought to be around 108 million years old. That's young for a Moon crater! Most are around 3.9 billion years old.

Sea of Tranquility

This large mare is surrounded by mountains. It was where Apollo 11, the mission in which humans first set foot on the Moon, landed in 1969.

Moon volcanoes

Billions of years ago, lava flowed on the surface of the Moon, just like it has throughout history on planet Earth. Most of the Moon's lava oozed up from beneath its surface through cracks, but some erupted from volcanoes.

Volcanic glass

The Moon has volcanoes that once spewed lava high above the surface. The lava quickly cooled in the cold vacuum of space, forming glass droplets. We know this because scientists analyzed the mysterious orange, green, and black glass beads in soil that astronauts brought back from the Moon. They discovered they were tiny beads of volcanic glass.

When the seeped lava cooled, it formed hard, dark rock.

Lava floods

Most lava on the Moon seeped out from cracks in the crust, filling low-lying regions such as craters and basins. This process is called flood volcanism, and is what made the Moon's vast, dark regions—the maria!

Some lava reached the surface through volcanic eruptions.

Lava tubes

On many rocky planets, including the Moon, lava often flows underground, melting its way through the crust and forming tunnels called lava tubes. When the lava stops flowing and drains away, the empty tubes become just like caves.

Collapsed lava tube

Collapsed lava tube

In the future, rovers could be controlled by astronauts on the edge of cave openings.

Caves on the Moon

Scientists have discovered openings to these caves on the surface of the Moon! The caves formed by lava tubes are big enough for humans to fit inside. This means that one day, people could live in these caves on the Moon.

Cave opening

Humans haven't yet explored caves on the Moon, but they are thinking about ways that they could.

What do you think it would be like to live in a Moon cave?

Large Moon rovers could drop smaller rovers into caves to explore.

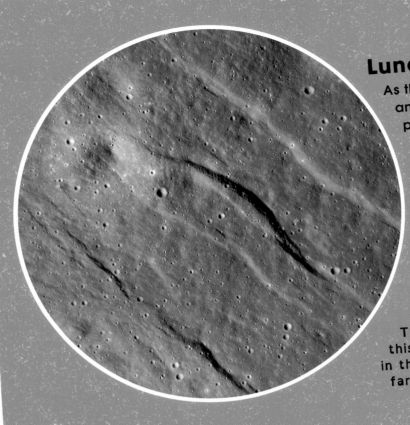

Lunar graben

As the Moon's surface stretches and expands, it sometimes pulls apart in places. This can cause the land to drop into the gap that is created, forming low trenches and valleys called lunar graben.

The lunar graben in this image are found in the highlands on the farside of the Moon.

The changing surface

Even now, 4.5 billion years after it first formed, the Moon's surface is still changing—craters form and its surface shrinks and wrinkles. Scientists believe that the Moon's core is still cooling down, causing its surface to change. These changes create interesting new features that are captured by telescopes and spacecraft for scientists to study and learn from. They show that the Moon is still an active world.

Lunar quakes

Apollo astronauts left seismometers (instruments that measure the movement of the ground) on the Moon in the 1960s and 1970s to detect moonquakes. Some of these quakes were probably related to the continued shrinking of the Moon, whereas others may have been caused by impacts.

Wrinkle ridges

These ridges can be found snaking across maria on the Moon. Scientists think they formed when lava that filled the maria cooled, causing the surface to tighten and shrink. The ridges can stretch as far as 250 miles (402 km) and rise as high as 1,000 ft (304 m).

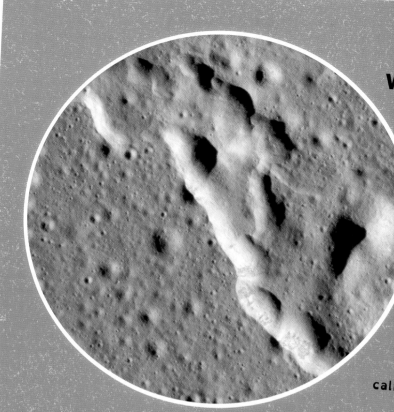

These wrinkle ridges are found in an area called the Mare Frigoris.

Lobate scarps

As the inside of the Moon has cooled over the years, it has shrunk in size. As a result, the crust on the Moon's surface has broken and overlapped, creating ridges called lobate scarps. These features can be found on other planets too, such as Mercury.

This image was taken near Mare Frigoris by the Lunar Reconnaissance Orbiter (LRO).

PAST, PRESENT, AND FUTURE EXPLORATION

The Moon is the most explored world in the solar system, other than Earth.

We have studied the Moon from Earth, sent robotic spacecraft to explore, and put humans on its surface. The exploration of the Moon continues to be one of our greatest achievements as humans, and the more we learn, the more questions we want to answer. In this section, you'll learn about some of the greatest discoveries about the Moon, and find out what the future holds for exploration.

A world beyond ours

When the Italian astronomer Galileo Galilei looked at the Moon with a telescope in 1609, he discovered that it had mountains, valleys, and what he thought were seas. He realized it was a world beyond our own.

Galileo created sketches of the Moon as he saw it through the telescope.

Supernatural sphere

Long before the telescope was invented in the 1600s, scientists and philosophers thought the Moon was a perfectly smooth glass sphere in the sky, or even a god. It did not occur to them that it could be another world.

The Moon through history

As technology has become more advanced, so has our understanding of the Moon. Imagine if you didn't know anything about the Moon—what would you think it was? People have explained the mysterious object in the sky in all sorts of different ways throughout history. For hundreds of years, traveling to the Moon was something only possible in stories, until scientists made the idea a reality!

Sea of Showers   Sea of Serenity

Sea of Tranquility

Sea of Tranquility

Ocean of Storms

Sea of Clouds

Shooting for the Moon

Before modern rockets were invented, French writer Jules Verne wrote a novel about three people being launched to the Moon in a cannon. It was called *From the Earth to the Moon* and was published in 1865.

Naming the seas

An old saying claims: "When the Moon is waxing the weather will be fine and when it is waning the weather will be cloudy, rainy, stormy, and generally unpleasant." The saying inspired astronomers Giovanni Riccioli and Francesco Grimaldi when they named the Moon's dark regions in the 1600s. They were the first people to create a labeled map of the Moon.

Rocket star

In 1920, American scientist Robert Goddard suggested using his new invention, the liquid-fueled rocket, to travel to the Moon. By 1926, he had built and flown his rocket. Although it didn't get to the Moon—in fact, it only flew up 41 ft (12.5 m)—it paved the way for rocket travel into space.

How spacecraft explore

It is easier and safer for spacecraft to venture into space than for people. Because of this, scientists use a variety of robotic spacecraft to explore the Moon. Each robotic spacecraft has a slightly different job, and together they help to build a complete picture. Some spacecraft fly above for an overhead view, while others touch down on the surface to collect data. Their findings are communicated back to Earth.

Flybys

Some robotic spacecraft only fly by the Moon briefly. In 1959, Luna 1 became the first spacecraft to fly past the Moon. In 2017, OSIRIS-REx flew past the Moon on its way to an asteroid.

Galileo

After it flew past the Moon, Galileo flew past all of Jupiter's major moons.

Liftoff!

All robotic spacecraft get to the Moon by rocket. Some of the biggest rockets in the world were built to travel to the Moon.

Rocket

Sample return

Rovers and landers sometimes carry equipment that let them launch rocks back to Earth for study in large laboratories.

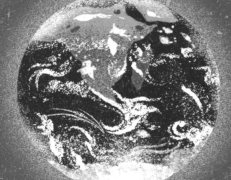

Earth

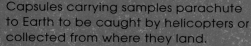

Capsules carrying samples parachute to Earth to be caught by helicopters or collected from where they land.

Orbiters

The best way to see a large amount of the Moon is to orbit it. Robotic spacecraft can spend years circling the Moon to capture pictures of each mountain and crater, with the Sun shining from every direction.

SELENE, also known as Kaguya

SELENE, an orbiter from Japan, studied the Moon's surface and its origins.

Impactors

Scientists don't just want to know what is on the surface of the Moon—they also want to find out what is beneath it. They do this by crashing things onto the surface and seeing what gets dug up!

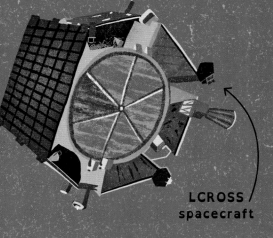

Centaur impactor

LCROSS deliberately crashed part of a rocket, called a Centaur, into the Moon. This was done to create a cloud of debris for the LCROSS spacecraft to fly through and collect data.

LCROSS spacecraft

Farside of the Moon

Landers and rovers

Touching the surface of the Moon is possible using landers and rovers. This allows scientists to get more detailed views of the surface, and also shows us what it is like on parts of the Moon that humans have not visited.

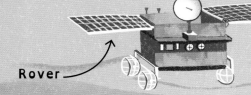

Rover

Rovers can move around to explore rocks and hillsides over larger areas.

Landers also study things such as radiation and moonquakes.

Lander

Seeing the farside of the Moon

The farside of the Moon looks very different than the side we see from Earth—there are fewer maria and many more craters. Scientists are still exploring why there are these differences.

Luna 3

Luna 3

The first ever mission to see the farside of the Moon was carried out by the USSR's spacecraft Luna 3 in 1959. It flew around the east side of the Moon and captured images of 70 percent of the farside. The photographs Luna 3 took were then transmitted back to Earth by radio after it began to orbit back toward its home planet.

Moon

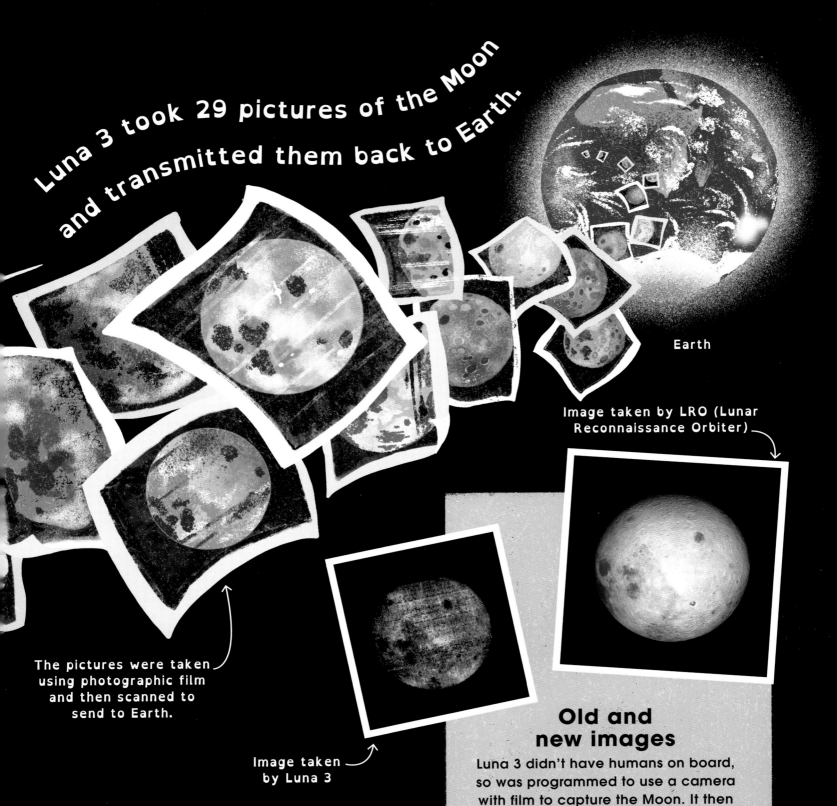

Luna 3 took 29 pictures of the Moon and transmitted them back to Earth.

Earth

Image taken by LRO (Lunar Reconnaissance Orbiter)

The pictures were taken using photographic film and then scanned to send to Earth.

Image taken by Luna 3

Until the Luna 3 mission, scientists thought that the farside of the Moon looked the same as the side seen from Earth.

Old and new images

Luna 3 didn't have humans on board, so was programmed to use a camera with film to capture the Moon. It then developed and scanned the photos, before sending them back to Earth as electric signals. Today, scientists use lightweight digital cameras, which are able to take much clearer images.

Getting closer to the Moon

Since the 1960s, we have sent spacecraft to look at the Moon in different ways from how we see it from Earth—to touch its surface and take pictures up close. Data from historic missions is still used for science and to plan future missions.

Ranger 7 took photos of the Moon's surface.

Ranger 7

The NASA-built space probe Ranger 7 launched on a rocket from the US in 1964. Ranger 7 took 4,308 images of the Moon before hitting its surface.

Juno 1 rocket

Juno 1

To get to the Moon, you first have to leave Earth. The first rocket to carry a satellite to space was the Juno 1 rocket in 1958. The satellite was the Explorer 1.

Luna 9

Launched by the USSR in 1966, Luna 9 was the first spacecraft to land in one piece on a space object. It showed scientists that the Moon's surface was solid and could support the weight of a lander—they had previously wondered if objects might sink into a layer of dust. It also took pictures of rocks and the Moon's landscape.

Lunar Orbiter 1

Lunar Orbiter 1 was launched by the US in 1966. Its aim was to take photographs of places where the Apollo missions could potentially land. With a huge camera weighing as much as an adult person, Lunar Orbiter 1 took photos of an area of the Moon that covered 2 million square miles (3.2 million km^2).

Surveyor 3

This craft, which launched in 1967, carried an instrument that could reach 5 ft (1.5 m) from the lander and dig 7 in (18 cm) deep. It was used to dig into and take samples of the surface of the Moon. A TV camera on board meant that scientists on Earth could see what the craft was discovering about the Moon's surface.

Apollo missions

In 1961, American president John F. Kennedy challenged the scientific and engineering community to land humans on the Moon before the end of the decade. By 1969, his dreams were realized by the Apollo program.

The lunar lander *Orion* brought the astronauts down to the Moon's surface.

The astronauts planted an American flag.

Mission timeline

Dec. 21–27, 1968

The first crewed flight of the Apollo program orbited the Moon ten times. These astronauts were the first to see the lunar farside firsthand.

Mar. 3–13, 1969

The lunar lander practiced docking with the command module as it orbited the Moon.

Jul. 16–24, 1969

Astronauts Armstrong and Aldrin were the first humans to walk on the Moon, while Collins orbited them in the sky above.

Nov. 14–24, 1969

Astronauts placed an Apollo Lunar Surface Experiments Package: scientific equipment that could study the Moon on its own.

Apr. 11–17, 1970

An oxygen tank failed and the mission had to return to Earth before landing on the Moon. NASA called it a "successful failure."

Apollo spacecraft

The Apollo missions were launched on the 36-stories-high Saturn V rocket. On top of its engines and tanks of rocket fuel, it carried a command module and a lunar lander. The command module orbited the Moon, while the lander carried astronauts to the surface.

Saturn V rocket

Command module

Lunar lander

This image is of the Apollo 16 mission on the Moon in 1972.

Astronaut John Young appears to hover above the ground after jumping upward. Astronaut Charles Duke is taking the picture.

Jan. 31–Feb. 9, 1971

Astronauts carried tree seeds into space. Some of them were planted back on Earth as "Moon Trees."

Jul. 26–Aug. 7, 1971

Astronauts used a Moon buggy to collect rocks. They also did experiments in orbit and launched a satellite.

Apr. 16–27, 1972

Astronauts collected the largest Moon rock ever brought back to Earth. Called "Big Muley," it weighed 26 lb (12 kg).

Dec. 7–19, 1972

Astronaut Harrison Schmitt was the first geologist to visit the Moon. He chose rocks to study back on Earth.

A day on the Moon

A day on the Moon lasts 29.5 days, or about one Earth month. Since one side of the Moon (the nearside) only ever faces Earth, if you are anywhere on the nearside, you will always see Earth. If you go to the farside, you will never see Earth. If you do see Earth, it will go through phases just like we see the Moon going through phases from Earth. Spending a day on the Moon would be very different from spending a day on Earth!

April

MON	TUE	WED	THU	FRI	S
🌑					

One month on Earth is the same length as one day on the Moon.

Imagine you're an astronaut on the Moon. What can you sense?

Smell
Astronauts have reported that lunar dust smells like gunpowder—not that you could take your helmet off to sniff!

See
Going to the Moon would be a bit like waking up in a black-and-white movie. Everything is shades of gray due to the rocks on the surface.

Hear
Without air, there is no sound on the Moon. Astronauts use radios to communicate with each other, since this does not require air.

Many days of day and night

A day lasts so long on the Moon that you would experience about two Earth weeks of daytime with the Sun in the sky and two weeks of nighttime with no Sunlight. When humans live on the Moon, we will have to find ways of adapting to long periods of time with only night or day.

Seeing stars

Unlike on Earth, on the Moon you can see distant stars both at night and in the daytime as long as you aren't looking at the Sun.

Sun

Feel

Moon rocks, dust, and sand are extremely sharp and would irritate your skin—you wouldn't want to touch it with your bare hands. You would also feel lighter due to there being less gravity than on Earth.

Taste

Astronauts living in space habitats report that food tastes more bland when they are there. You might want to bring some spices to space!

Moon rocks on Earth

Scientists can study the Moon by analyzing rocks that have traveled the long distance from there to Earth. These rocks have journeyed to Earth in different ways—some were collected by the Apollo astronauts in the 1960s, and others came from robotic sample return missions. Scientists know where these rocks were collected on the Moon. However, some rocks have traveled to Earth as lunar meteorites and come from unknown places. Scientists can use these rocks to investigate what the Moon is made of, how it was formed, and its history.

In the lab
Researchers on Earth must be very careful to protect any rocks collected from the Moon. This is to make sure our environment doesn't change the rocks.

Apollo mission samples
The Apollo astronauts collected 2,200 rock and soil samples from the Moon, weighing a total of 842 lb (382 kg). They were taken back to Earth so scientists could study the lunar surface.

Moon rocks can teach us about the history and chemistry of the places they came from.

Crash!

Sometimes rocks from outer space crash into the Moon. But these impacts don't just make craters on the Moon's surface—they can also fling pieces of the Moon out into space. Sometimes these pieces of Moon rock, called lunar meteorites, make it all the way to Earth.

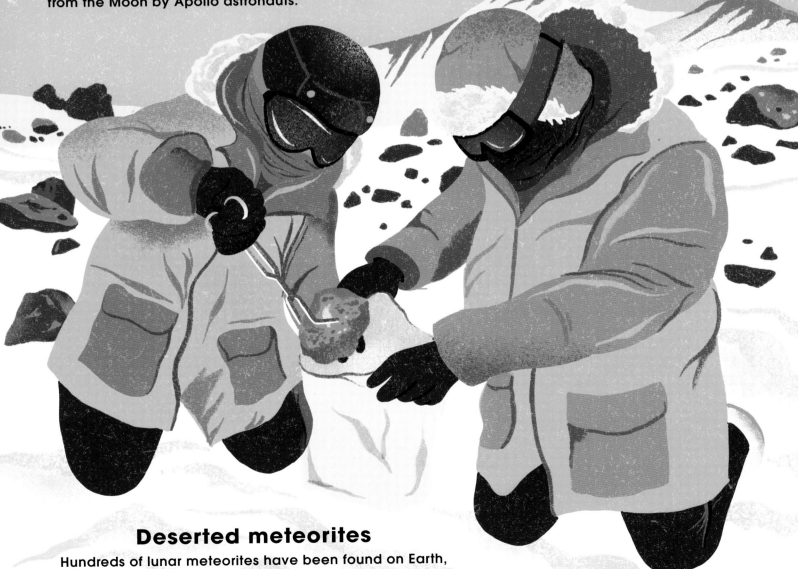

Rock from outer space

Moon

Lunar rock

The Moon in Antarctica

In 1982, a meteorite found on Earth in Antarctica was discovered to be from the Moon! When the rock was analyzed, scientists found that how it was made up was similar to rocks brought to Earth from the Moon by Apollo astronauts.

Deserted meteorites

Hundreds of lunar meteorites have been found on Earth, and most of them were found in deserts. They came from unknown places from all over the Moon.

Mapping the Moon

Many spacecraft are taking photos of the Moon in incredible detail. They have also mapped it using laser, radar, and other instruments. This has helped us to understand everything from where the Moon is hot and cold, to where the biggest holes and highest mountains are found.

LRO

Topographical map

In 1994, NASA's Clementine mission mapped the entire Moon in detail for the first time. One instrument mapped the elevation (height of the ground). This map revealed the largest impact basin, South Pole-Aitken, on the farside for the first time. This was the best topographic map of the Moon for 15 years—until the LRO mission in 2009.

Gravity map

The GRAIL mission mapped variations in the Moon's surface gravity to understand what was below the surface. It used twin spacecraft named Ebb and Flow. The crafts would constantly communicate where they were. When Ebb passed over a place with stronger gravity, it would get pulled closer to the surface, and would let Flow know that they were farther from each other. Then they could tell Earth scientists how far they were from Earth.

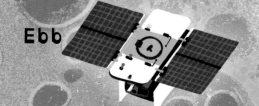

Ebb

Flow

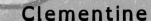

Clementine

Compositional map

Clementine had special cameras that could see types of light that human eyes cannot see, such as infrared. It helped to make this map with both visible light and infrared light. Scientists matched the colors Clementine saw with the colors of known rocks in the lab. This helped them figure out what was on the surface, so they could make compositional maps of the entire surface of the Moon. This is a map of iron on the lunar surface.

Elements map

Lunar Prospector was the first mission to map the location of certain elements on the entire lunar surface. It was looking for resources on the Moon. For the first time, we could see that the Moon's largest dark spot was rich in radioactive elements such as uranium and thorium. People are working to better understand radiation on the Moon, which may be harmful to future human explorers.

Lunar Prospector

Water detector

LRO has a special instrument called the Lunar Explorer Neutron Detector (LEND), which has helped scientists to detect water on the Moon.

LEND

LEND scanned the lunar south pole to measure how much hydrogen was in the soil, creating the map above. The areas with hydrogen are blue. Hydrogen is one of the two chemical elements that make up water. This is a useful hint that water may exist in the places where hydrogen is found.

Water on the Moon

One of the most exciting recent discoveries about the Moon has been finding water on its surface. The more we explore the surface, the better we can plan for sending humans to explore and build a long-term presence there. For example, scientists have learned that some of the craters near the north and south poles never get sunlight, making them extremely cold. In their shadows, there may be large deposits of water ice that humans could someday use to live on the Moon.

Impactor

In 2009, the Lunar Crater Observation and Sensing Satellite (LCROSS) was used to find water on the Moon. First, a piece of the rocket was sent to smash into a crater near the south pole. Then, LCROSS flew through the debris to study it and send information back to Earth. Four minutes later, LCROSS also crashed into the Moon.

LCROSS hitting the Moon

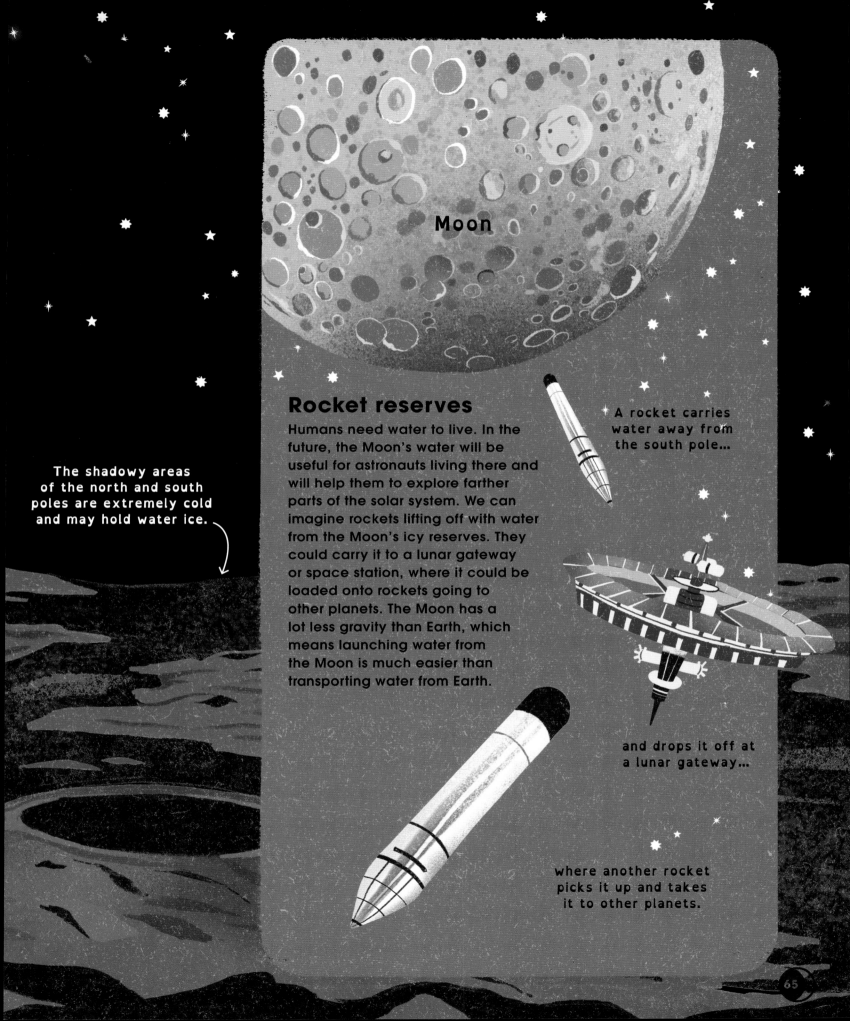

Moon

The shadowy areas of the north and south poles are extremely cold and may hold water ice.

Rocket reserves

Humans need water to live. In the future, the Moon's water will be useful for astronauts living there and will help them to explore farther parts of the solar system. We can imagine rockets lifting off with water from the Moon's icy reserves. They could carry it to a lunar gateway or space station, where it could be loaded onto rockets going to other planets. The Moon has a lot less gravity than Earth, which means launching water from the Moon is much easier than transporting water from Earth.

A rocket carries water away from the south pole...

and drops it off at a lunar gateway...

where another rocket picks it up and takes it to other planets.

Ongoing discoveries about the Moon

The task of exploring the Moon and learning new things about its surface and environment will never be finished. It is taking a global fleet of spacecraft, landers, and robots to prepare the way for humans to return to this fascinating other world in our sky.

Looking to the future...

Scientists and engineers will send more and more instruments to further explore the Moon. These will include seismometers, different types of cameras, and rovers. They are also sending new technology to test ahead of more human exploration on the Moon.

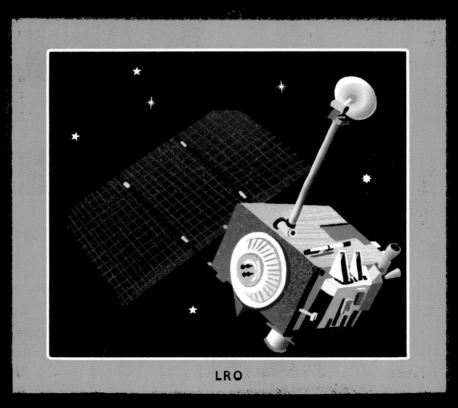

LRO

Lunar Reconnaissance Orbiter

Nicknamed LRO, this is a Moon-mapping machine. It has many different instruments that let researchers measure the heights and depths of the lunar surface and take images of every detail. It has a camera that is so powerful that it can see the trails left by Apollo astronauts walking and driving around.

Chandrayaan Series

Indian Space Research Organization (ISRO) missions started visiting the Moon in 2008. The first launch included both an orbiter and an impactor that studied water on the Moon. Each additional flight is testing more advanced technologies, with the aim of exploring the lunar south pole with a lander and a rover.

Chandrayaan Series

Chang'e Series

In 2007, Chinese spacecraft Chang'e 1 began mapping the Moon to prepare for future landers. It was followed by Chang'e 2, which had higher resolution cameras, and Chang'e 3, with landers and rovers. In 2018, Chang'e 4's Yutu 2 became the first rover to land on the farside of the Moon. To communicate to Earth, it relays signals through a communications satellite called Queqiao. The satellite sits beyond the Moon where it can see Earth and the Moon's farside. In 2020, Chang'e 5 put a lander on the surface that gathered rocks to bring back to Earth for scientists to study. Additional missions will gather more rocks and search for water ice at the south pole.

Chang'e Series

Understanding other worlds

Studying the surface of the Moon is important in helping us learn more about other rocky objects in the solar system. For example, the way craters form on rocky worlds is pretty much the same from place to place—just the shapes and sizes can be a bit different. We have learned that these differences are related to what each world is made of, how much gravity it has, and what its atmosphere is like, if it has one.

The Moon

All space rocks that hit the Moon form craters. Even dust can make tiny craters! This is because the Moon doesn't have an atmosphere. This also means there is no wind or weather to wipe away marks once they are made.

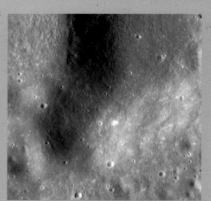

The young surface of the Moon

Close-up craters

One of the most important things we can learn from these worlds is the history of the solar system. Each world has been hit by space rocks of many sizes at a similar rate for most of the solar system's history. This means that land with a lot of craters is old, and where there are fewer craters, the land is younger.

The old surface of the Moon

Mercury

Looking at Mercury's surface, we can see many more cracks than we can see on the Moon. This tells us that it is shrinking more than the Moon. A good example of these cracks can be seen in Goethe Basin, a particularly large crater. You can also see wrinkle ridges and valleys.

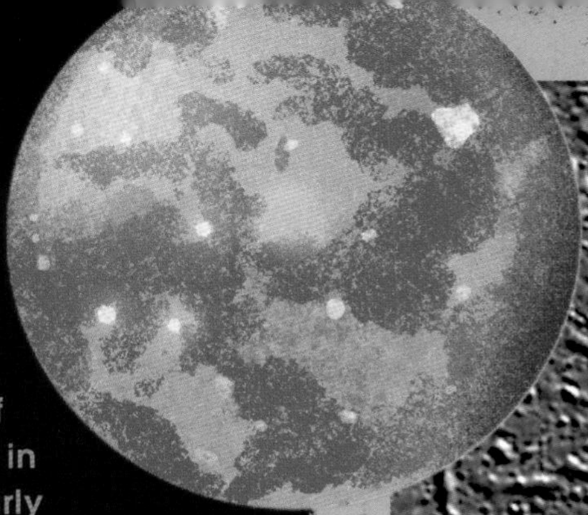

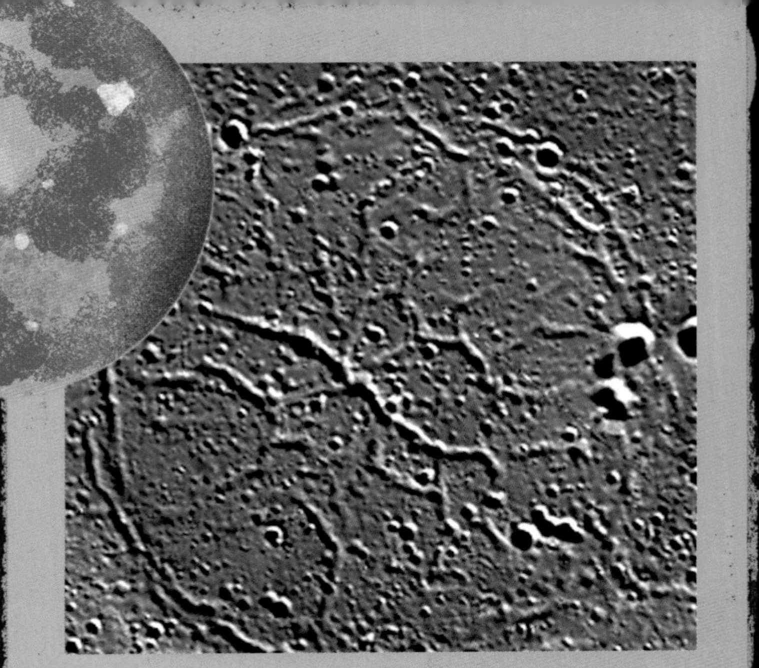

Cracks in Goethe Basin

Mars

Very tiny craters and really large basins are much less common on Mars than the Moon. This is because Mars has a thin atmosphere that burns up incoming meteoroids—big meteoroids get smaller before they hit, and very small meteoroids get burned up completely before they reach the ground. This image shows Jezero crater, which scientists think may have been flooded with water at one time.

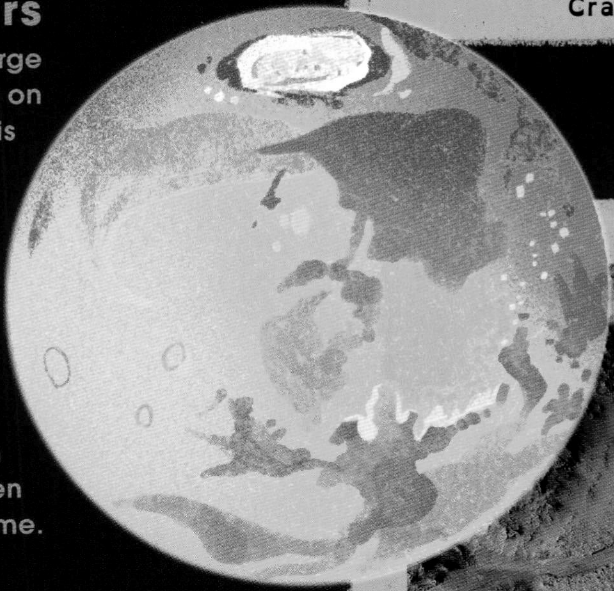

Jezero crater

Moon craters can tell us much about other worlds.

The people who explore

No single person can know everything about the Moon, its landscape, and how to stay alive on its surface.

Scientists hope that one day there will be a small station of humans on the Moon, supported by thousands of other people back down on Earth, all connected by technology. This dream will only be achieved with the help of many people with many different skills. There is a lot to be done—from planning and training for each mission, to designing experiments and preparing meals to keep everyone healthy.

No matter what you're interested in, there is probably a career related to space that can use your skills. Some careers will lead you to college, where you can study your chosen subject for many years, while others are trades that you learn working alongside skilled craftspeople.

Computer scientist

Every aspect of space exploration is controlled by technology. Computer scientists are the people who research, plan, and write the instructions that make technology work.

Hardware engineer

All around us are machines such as computers that can process information and perform tasks related to the Moon. Hardware engineers have the job of designing all their physical parts.

Medical doctor

People can get sick or hurt anywhere—even on the Moon. Doctors keep astronauts healthy and check that they are well enough to go on missions into space. They also study how the Moon affects the body.

Lunar geologist

Lunar geologists are specialists that study the Moon's landscape and what it is made of. They look closely at images, data, and rocks to figure out how the Moon formed and changed over time.

Architect

People need places to work and live in any world, and it is up to architects to design these places so they are both useful and comfortable. Future buildings on the Moon will be designed by architects.

Astronaut

If you do any of these jobs in space, you are an astronaut! As well as flying spacecraft, astronauts do jobs and experiments in space, and each astronaut on a mission has a specific role to perform.

Humans on the Moon

The Moon is our next great stopping point as we continue our adventures in space. Once a permanent base has been built on the Moon, humans will be able to live there. Living in space will be difficult and dangerous, but it will be possible. One day, books will be written about the first explorers who built the first human places that made life on the Moon a reality.

Will you be one of the first people in history to make a home on a world beyond our own?

Digging in the dirt

Geologists and planetary scientists are eager to dig into the Moon's surface to look for new types of minerals to study. They also hope to find resources, such as building materials or chemicals, for us to use.

Shadows are darker on the Moon, so flashlights are very useful.

Robots will be used to carry tools to the field, and rocks back for study.

Space ferries

Today, we're using small spacecraft called capsules to carry supplies and people to space stations. Future astronauts may use capsules to travel between space stations near the Moon and Earth, using them a bit like ferries in space.

Landers may fly people from space stations to the Moon's surface and back.

Upright solar panels will be needed near the Moon's poles to capture the Sun's energy and provide power to humans on the Moon.

Some rovers will be like lunar RVs, with places for people to sleep, for multiday trips.

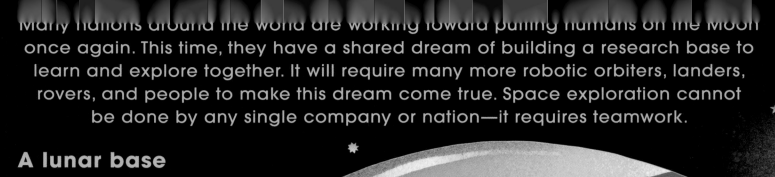

Many nations around the world are working toward putting humans on the Moon once again. This time, they have a shared dream of building a research base to learn and explore together. It will require many more robotic orbiters, landers, rovers, and people to make this dream come true. Space exploration cannot be done by any single company or nation—it requires teamwork.

A lunar base

The permanent research base on the Moon would be a lot like the ones we have in Antarctica on Earth, where people go to live and work for months at a time.

Craters could be turned into buildings.

What do you think a habitat on the Moon would look like?

Metal mined from lunar rocks could be used to build buildings and spacecraft.

There is no air on the Moon, so visitors would have to wear a spacesuit just to go outside.

Get involved!

Calling all aspiring Moon explorers! With study, hard work, creativity, and perseverance, you could be part of the team building our future on the Moon. It will take a diverse group of specialists to make living on the Moon a success.

Space stations could act as stopovers to and from Earth.

No one really knows what a city on the Moon would look like as it doesn't exist yet! Use your imagination to make up your own.

The Moon would be a stopping point for missions to Mars and beyond.

Batteries may provide power during the two-week-long nights.

Car makers on Earth could partner with space programs to develop more lunar rovers.

Water trapped as ice in the Moon's shadowy craters could be used for rocket fuel.

Lots and lots of solar panels could charge batteries to power a moonbase.

Underground homes could be built in lava tubes and caves.

GLOSSARY

Apollo Program
Spaceflight program run by NASA in the US from 1961 to 1972, which carried out the first crewed Moon landing

asteroid
Small, rocky object that orbits the Sun

astronomer
Person who studies space and things in space

atmosphere
Layer of gases that surrounds a planet dwarf planet, or moon—a number of moons have atmospheres

axis
Imaginary line that passes through the center of a planet or star, around which the planet or star rotates

celestial
To do with space

comet
Object made of ice and dust that orbits around the Sun, developing a tail when it is near to the Sun

diameter
Distance through the center of a circle or sphere from one side to the opposite side

eclipse
When an object in space passes into the shadow of another object

farside
Side of the Moon that can't be seen from Earth

Gaia
Larger of the two planets that collided billions of years ago to form Earth

gravity
Invisible force that pulls objects toward each other

high tide
When the sea level is at its highest

low tide
When the sea level is at its lowest

mass
Measurement of how much matter is in an object

meteor
When a meteoroid burns up as it enters Earth's atmosphere, appearing as a streak of light

meteorite
Meteoroid that lands on a planet or moon's surface

meteoroid
Small rock in space that has broken off from a bigger space rock

NASA
National Aeronautics and Space Administration, a US agency dedicated to the study of space science

nearside
Side of the Moon that can be seen from Earth

orbit
Path a celestial object takes around another due to gravity, such as how planets travel around the Sun

orbiter
Spacecraft designed to fly around a Moon or planet without landing on it

probe
Unmanned spacecraft designed to study objects in space and send information back to Earth

radius
Distance from the center to the edge of a circle or sphere

rover
Vehicle for exploring the surface of a planet or moon

seismometer
Instrument that measures the movements of the ground

solar panel
Surface that creates electricity from the energy in sunlight

spacecraft
Vehicle that travels in space

spherical
Round in shape

telescope
Tool used to look at objects very far away

terrestrial
Relating to Earth

Theia
Smaller of the two planets that collided billions of years ago to form Earth

USSR
Union of Soviet Socialist Republics, also known as the Soviet Union, a Russian-led communist group of countries

vacuum
Volume with nothing in it—not even air

volume
Space taken up by an object or vaccuum

waning
Phases of the Moon where the Moon appears to shrink because we are seeing less of the Sunlit side

waxing
Phases of the Moon where the Moon appears to grow because we are seeing more of the Sunlit side

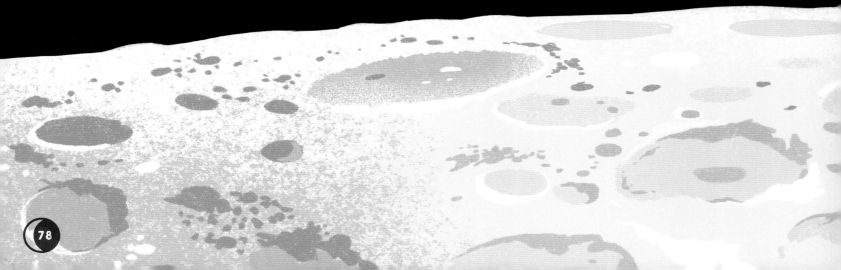

ACKNOWLEDGMENTS

DK would like to thank Laura Gilbert for the index and Agey George and Jackie Hornberger for proofreading. Special thanks to the Planetary Science Institute for their endless knowledge and expertise.

The publisher would like to thank the following for their kind permission to reproduce their photographs:

(Key: a-above; b-below/bottom; c-center; f-far; l-left; r-right; t-top)

1 NASA: GSFC / Arizona State University. **11 NASA**: Goddard Space Flight Center Scientific Visualization Studio (crb). **12 Alamy Stock Photo**: NG Images (c). **Dreamstime.com**: Patrimonio Designs Limited / Patrimonio (cra). **13 NASA**: GSFC / Arizona State University (cb); JPL (cr); JPL / University of Arizona (cl). **14 NASA**: GSFC / Arizona State University (c). **16 Dreamstime.com**: Idreamphotos (bc). **16-17 Getty Images / iStock**: RomoloTavani (b). **Science Photo Library**: Eckhard Slawik (t). **18-19 Science Photo Library**: Eckhard Slawik. **20 Science Photo Library**: Eckhard Slawik (cr). **21 Science Photo Library**: Eckhard Slawik (tc, cra). **26-27 Dreamstime.com**: Scol22 (ca); Vladvitek (b). **32 Dreamstime.com**: Siimsepp (br). **33 Shutterstock.com**: topseller (cra). **34 Science Photo Library**: Damian Peach (cra). **35 NASA**: Goddard Space Flight Center (tr). **38 Alamy Stock Photo**: Novo Images / Glasshouse Images (bl). **39 Alamy Stock Photo**: Cristian Cestaro (cr); NASA Image Collection (br). **40-41 Alamy Stock Photo**: Brian Kushner. **41 Alamy Stock Photo**: Robin Scagell / Galaxy Picture Library (crb); Rolf Geissinger / Stocktrek Images (ca). **NASA**: Goddard Space Flight Center / Arizona State University (cra); GFSC / Arizona State University (cb). **43 NASA**: Arizona State University (cra); Goddard / Arizona State University (cr). **44 NASA**: (crb); Goddard / Arizona State University / Smithsonian Institution (tl). **45 NASA**: (t); Goddard Space Flight Center (b). **48 Alamy Stock Photo**: Stocktrek Images (cra). **49 Alamy Stock Photo**: Brian Kushner (cla). **53 NASA**: Goddard Space Flight Center Scientific Visualization Studio (cb,cr). **54 NASA**: JPL-Caltech (cla). **Science Photo Library**: NASA (cl). **55 Alamy Stock Photo**: NASA Image Collection (br). **NASA**: (cl). **Science Photo Library**: Detlev Van Ravenswaay (tr). **56 NASA**: (tl, cla, cl, clb, bl). **56-57 Shutterstock.com**: Digital Images Studio. **57 NASA**: (cra, cr, crb, br). **58 NASA**: GSFC / Arizona State University (cra). **60 NASA**: David Scott (cl). **62 NASA**: Goddard Space Flight Center / DLR / ASU (cl); JPL-Caltech / MIT / GSFC (br). **63 Alamy Stock Photo**: Granger - Historical Picture Archvie (cla). **Science Photo Library**: NASA (br). **64 NASA**: Goddard Space Flight Center (cla). **66 Alamy Stock Photo**: Konrad Wothe / Image Professionals GmbH (tl). **68 NASA**: Arizona State University (crb, clb); Johnson Space Center (br); GSFC / Arizona State University (cra). **69 NASA**: Johns Hopkins University / APL (tr). **Shutterstock.com**: mkarco (crb)

Cover images: Front: **Dorling Kindersley**: Natural History Museum, London crb; **Dreamstime.com**: Reinhold Wittich crb/ (Comet); **NASA**: cra; **Science Photo Library**: Carlos Clarivan cla; Back: **Dreamstime.com**: Nerthuz bl, Reinhold Wittich cra; **Science Photo Library**: Eckhard Slawik (Moon); Spine: **Dreamstime.com**: Nerthuz b

All other images © Dorling Kindersley

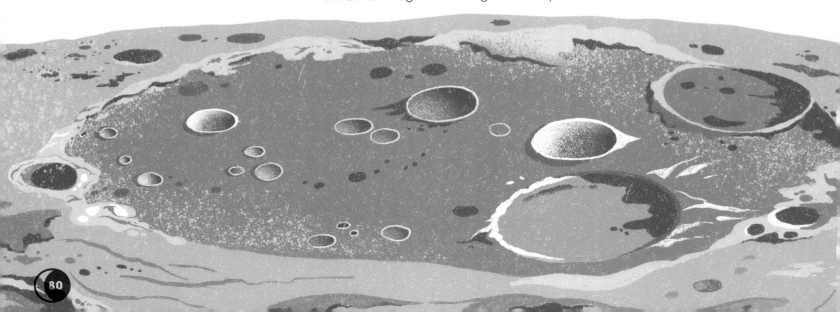